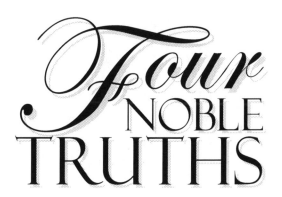

Four NOBLE TRUTHS

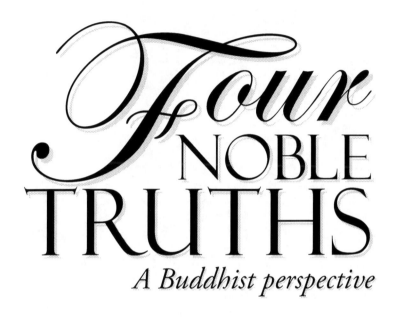

Four NOBLE TRUTHS

A Buddhist perspective

SAYADAW U KHEMA WUNTHA

iUniverse

FOUR NOBLE TRUTHS
A BUDDHIST PERSPECTIVE

iUniverse books may be ordered through booksellers or by contacting:

iUniverse
1663 Liberty Drive
Bloomington, IN 47403
www.iuniverse.com
1-800-Authors (1-800-288-4677)

Because of the dynamic nature of the Internet, any web addresses or links contained in this book may have changed since publication and may no longer be valid. The views expressed in this work are solely those of the author and do not necessarily reflect the views of the publisher, and the publisher hereby disclaims any responsibility for them.

Any people depicted in stock imagery provided by Thinkstock are models, and such images are being used for illustrative purposes only. Certain stock imagery © Thinkstock.

ISBN: 978-1-4917-5292-0 (sc)
ISBN: 978-1-4917-5293-7 (e)

Printed in the United States of America.

iUniverse rev. date: 11/24/2014

Contents

Dedications

The most Venerable Sayadaw U Pannya Vamsa, Chief Monk of Dhammikarama Burmese Buddhist Temple, Penang, Malaysia, my preceptor and teacher who give me inspiration, support and guidance. The profound teaching about the nature of human beings, the life, Buddhism and all topic transmitting me (Oral Teaching) mostly after breakfast and lunch, at the table, is immeasurable guidance. I bow down and pay respect to my teacher always.

My parents who has given me unconditional Love. *This book is for them.*

Special thanks to the following devotees who believe in me and have supported and assisted me in the publication of this book:

(1) Jessie Lim and family from Penang, Malaysia.

(2) Lim Pau Lin and family from Singapore.

(3) Ooi Kim Ean and family from Penang, Malaysia.

(4) *Dhamma* brothers and sisters from the 'Chempaka Buddhist Lodge', Kuala Lumpur, Malaysia.

(5) Swas @ Teik Ee Tan from Penang, Malaysia for his support, suggestions, designing the book up to the final editing to

bring this book to its completion, without which it would not be possible to finish this book.

(6) Yeap Theam Kwee and Jenny Tan from Penang, Malaysia for final proofreading and assisting in the publication.

(7) Finally to all the devotees and friends who have helped me in one way or another and all donors for the publication of this book.

Well done. Much appreciation.

Sādhu! Sādhu! Sādhu!

May the merits accrued from

this *Dhamma-Dāna* be shared

with all sentient beings!

Foreword

SWAS TAN

"Life is no straight and easy corridor along which we travel free and unhampered but a maze of passages through which we must seek our way, lost and confused, new and again checked in a blind alley." wrote AJ Cronin. All of us can easily attest to this fact but we need not be "lost and confused" when we meet with a wise teacher whose teaching can point us the true way.

I am very fortunate and privileged to come across such a teacher, Sayadaw U Khema, by chance at Dhammikarama Buddhist Temple in Penang on June 11 2009. His talk on "On what grounds does Buddhism stand on?" caught my attention and interest. He spoke with simple gestures and direct to the point that many dismissed as something heard numerous times before, therefore missing the essence and profoundability of the Buddha's teachings. At that time, I had been compiling the *One Page Dhamma* and only after several personal dialogues with Sayadaw could it be possible for me to write accurately without missing the forest for the trees. Sayadaw's teachings have been primarily focused on the "Illusion of 'I' and how we can free ourselves from this entrapment. He constantly emphasized that Buddhism is about understanding all the realities within us and around us and for us to verity the Truth. When we do not get the instruction of what to do there is simply too wide an area to practise. Besides giving practical instructions on how to practise, Sayadaw reminded us on the importance of discipline "When I can't sit, I stay with that "can't sit", when I can sit, I stay with that "can sit". This constancy of effort allows us to stay in the unconditional acceptance of the present moment. A simple motto to remember is that when we react, the end result is always wrong.

I am extremely pleased that Sayadaw Khema gave me an opportunity to edit one of his previous books *"Buddhism and Liberation."* That was my first editing experience. Sayadaw was patient enough to answer all my questions and kind enough to approve a work that in my opinion, he could easily find someone who could have done a better job.

What you are holding in your hands is another opportunity given to me by Sayadaw Khema to edit. Deep and profound is the subject on the *Four Noble Truths*, it was a challenge to edit without misinterpreting the words of someone with deep and wide ranging experience.

The Buddha expounded the first discourse, *Turning the Wheel of the Dhamma (Dhammacakkappavattana Sutta),* a discourse primarily focused on suffering and the end of suffering. It is said that all other discourses are but a subset of this discourse. So as Buddhists it is our duty to fully understand this important teaching.

Today we are very fortunate to have the teachings of the Buddha so easily available to us through books, audios and videos and the Internet. This is an indication that Dhamma is still very much alive in the hearts of those who practise and wishing to share with others.

If the path of our practice is the path of observing life simply and directly, we have to learn by looking within. In the *Four Noble Truths*, you will find a set of teachings for developing and deepening meditation aimed particularly at suffering and end of suffering. Sayadaw offers a careful and subtle understanding of each of the Noble Truths, to transform our initial difficulties and how to incline the mind towards the natural state. These are beautiful teachings.

The First Noble Truth of Suffering must be understood. The Second Noble Truth of Cause of Suffering must be abandoned. The Third Noble Truth of the Cessation of Suffering must be realized. The Forth Noble Truth of the Way leading to the End of Suffering must be cultivated. Sayadaw Khema teaches us the essence of this teaching from his own experience. It is only when we practise that we can begin to understand the path, the pathless path that Sayadaw is talking about in this book. When we truly understand, it will have enduring significance and they always will be the foundation for your very own realization.

The Dhamma is beautiful in the beginning, beautiful in the middle and beautiful in the end. As you weave through the pages, learning to see deeply, opening your hearts more fully, acting with clarity and compassion you will, to a great extent, resonate with what Sayadaw Khema is saying. This book is not for intellectual reading but to assist you in your practice

May this book bring you closer to the Dhamma, pave the path for your practice and help you to navigate through this spiritual journey without being lost and confused.

Sincere Request

Please read my book with an open mind. Use your common sense and intelligence. Let the words be your inner voice as you read and not as fixed ideas in your mind.

There are two ways in studying and practicing Buddhism.

(1) Learning and studying (or teaching) like a Scholar or Researcher - Academically.

(2) Penetrate and see the things as they are. Intuitive knowledge. You need to quiet the mind - need meditation (more so in this era) to quiet the mind - Spiritually.

Best way is to do both in the "balance way"

Truly there was indeed a Historical Buddha and Historical Buddhism which is the authentic Buddhism. After the Buddha passed away, a span of more than 2500 years, Man-made (Teachers and scholars) Buddhism develops and we lost the essence of Buddhism. So I request that you read this book from the lens of a Historical Buddha and Historical Buddhism, not the Man-made Buddhism. In other words use your common sense and intelligence. Some of the topics that cannot be verified, we can leave them aside. Instead of speculating whether they are true or otherwise, we can leave them aside for now, not dismissing them or blindly subscribing to them. We can be totally honest with what we know and what we do not know.

This book Four Noble Truths, taught by the Buddha is meant to be understood "Spiritually". So I say again, use your common sense and intelligence, more so with the quiet and open mind.

It is a Fact

There is an unenlightened side (Mundane – Worldly – Lokiya) and also an enlightened side (Lokuttara – Supramundane leading up to Liberation state)

Unenlightened side:-

Human beings born and die, and in between we suffer – one way or another. We perceive there is the Devil, the Satan, and the Evil on one side. This perception is created (and projected) in our own mind by our own defilements - and condition(s) - (Greed, Hatred and Delusion). We place limitations upon ourselves, the feeling of insecurity, fear and confusion. And we created (and projected) an image and perceive that there is God, some kind of a Super Beings, Who promises to protect us and offer us security and eternality in some heavenly place. This perception is created by our own defilements also (Greed and 'For Me'). We surrender our authority to him, we pray for his protection and blessings to be in his favor.

(Note:- I am only referring to the state (of mind) created and projected by our limited and conditioned mind, not the 'Higher Source' or 'Liberation' which is not created and projected by our limited and conditioned mind)

These apparent forces, good and evil, fight against each other more so in the name of religion. We are caught in this dilemma since time immemorial, playing the roles of either being the good or the bad. This duality of living obstructs the mind from the possibility of liberation.

We live and die in this state never touch or truly understand the Liberation state.

Enlightened (Liberation) side: -

The Enlightened state is free from dualities and concepts, It is out of the above unenlightened side. This supramundane side is not created by our fears and insecurity. It is the unconditioned state; there is no constructs or fabrications of the limited mind. ***This 'state' is not created or projected by the mind.***

The Fact *(THE TRUTH)* is :-

So long as we continue to surrender our authority and potential to someone else, we can never be free. How can we be free if we are dependent on someone or something for our happiness? The limitations of life are present at conception. The fear and insecurity are not caused by the conditioning but by the decision we ourselves choose based on that conditioning. When we recognize this, we reclaim back our authority and we can choose to break away from the false identification of the limited self. This doesn't mean that we live a life of an ascetic and have nothing to do with the rest of the world. We depend on spiritual friends and wise teachers to show us the way, the right knowledge. Good intention and effort is not good enough, we need the right knowledge (right view) to be able to see through the fear and insecurity that is just an illusion. Then we can come out of our limited state.

This is the Fact. The Buddha taught us what he himself had practiced and realized – the Four Noble Truths. Suffering and the cause of suffering is not outside us, so we do not need to depend on someone to liberate us. The Buddha said that liberation is possible and he offered us the way to the cessation of all suffering - the Eightfold Noble Path. The fourth noble truth is to be practiced and cultivated. When we do that, we see clearly what are the causes and conditions that lead to our unhappiness and what truly lead to our happiness. This clarity of mind provides the vision and knowledge for liberation for then we can choose the causes that lead to happiness and abandon the causes that lead to unhappiness or suffering.

Many paths, many platform, many traditions, many teachers (in this era) but the fact still remains:-

(1) Limited and conditioned mind cannot touch or feel the Higher Source or Liberation *(Nibbana)* – whatever the name ones put. Have to get out or get rid of the limited and conditioned mind.

(2) Have to touch or feel the nature of Higher Source or Liberation.

(3) Take the Spiritual Journey (to Liberation)

Prelude

In my book 'Buddhism and Liberation' I pointed out that there are two conditions that we human beings encounter - The Natural Condition and the Man-made condition. The natural conditions are those that we cannot control, they happen when the right causes and conditions are there. Examples are old age, sickness and death. The Buddha passed away with old age and diarrhea is an example of natural condition. We take care of these natural condition. The Man-made condition on the other hand, is something that we intentionally do. All actions have consequences. This is the law of cause and effect or the *Law of Kamma*. It is this second condition that we must understand and be free from it.

In my previous books, I pointed out that defilements and the identification of self (what's in for me) is what traps us in suffering from the time of our ancestors and beginning-less time. The "Illusion of I" or *"Atta"* runs as the forefront in all our thought processes.

Now we will see that there are two sets of 'Self' in ourselves.

(1) The sense of 'self'. This is the normal, natural kind of self. 'I think therefore I am' said by **René Descartes.** He is perhaps best known for the philosophical statement "*Cogito ergo sum*" (French: *Je pense, donc je suis*; English: *I think,*

therefore I am; or I am thinking, therefore I exist or I do think, therefore I do exist).

(Latest joke – but quite true is the post-journalism existentialist "I blog, therefore I am".

This natural sense of self is what enables us to live and survive in the world. When we are hungry we eat; when we are tired, we sleep. We know we are human beings among the other beings; we know who our father or my mother is and so on. This is the natural self - the normal knowing and functioning of body and mind. We think, speak, hear, smell and taste normally. We follow the rules, regulation and protocols as a human beings, which is different from animals. This 'knowing' and 'functioning' is a kind of self that we live and function. When we are in deep sleep, there is no sense of 'self', but the moment we wake up and aware, this sense of self is there (It should be there, if not we fall down to low species)

> This kind of self is part and parcel of the body and mind. The body and mind assist this kind of self to function. The dignity, the protocols, language are the necessary items when this kind of 'sense of self' communicate among human beings. (You and I, job title and so on are the sense of self that let us understand each other and function in the world) This sense of self has nothing to do with the Big Ego, Entity, *ATTA* or Illusion of 'I', pointed in Buddhism. It is just a normal functioning as a human being, the natural action and response from being a human being.
>
> Note: - There is no way to find out who this sense of self is. Who created it, how does it exist? We take it as it is. This sense of self together with the natural condition (see above) functions until we die.

When the Buddha, as a prince was born, the sense of self – *as a prince*, together with the natural condition(s) were there and when He became a Buddha, sense of self – *as a Buddha*, together with the natural condition(s) were there. But there is no Man-made condition – from his part. He lived with the natural conditions (occasionally with the back pain) and passed away with the natural condition - diarrhea.

This is the Natural Self Awareness or Survival Identity.

(You can easily find the 'sense of self' in psychological teachings and in the internet)

(2) The second kind of 'Self' is the one I mention as 'Illusion of 'I'. It is the *'ATTA'* 'For Me' state in the mind. The Buddha pointed out *'ANATTA'* – Non Self' – in our body and mind, but if we are not enlightened we function with this kind 'Self'. There is a kind of fixed entity inside; we may refer this as the 'big ego', 'For Me', Illusion of 'I'. This is the 'EGO centered Self'.

This 'Self' is also part and parcel inside us. We developed it, handed down by our ancestor(s) and it becomes our second nature, a Man-made one. Because of this 'Self' – 'For Me' state, we react, we fabricate and we suffer. According to Buddhism, this is *Kamma* – Volitional action that traps us in the continuous cycle of the 31 existences. (See my book 'Buddhism and Liberation')

These cause and effect drama started from our ancestor(s) in repeated cycles from one generation to another and we wrongly identify and bear up with it. One Buddhism teacher from Penang, Malaysia (Brother Hor Kwei Loon) describes this as 'The mirage of ownership'.

This is the Self Centered Awareness or 'For Me' Awareness.

The 'Sense of self' and the 'Nature Condition' are our true nature, but when this second kind of Self – the illusion of 'I' sets in, we have moved from our true nature to the wrong kind of functioning which Buddhism points out as 'Suffering'. The Buddha was free from suffering and lived with the sense of self and the nature condition until He passed away.

> There is 'Suffering', from the moment we are born. We learn this wrong kind of functioning from our parents and neighbors and they got the idea from their parents all the way from our first ancestor(s). Now we hand down intentionally or unintentionally to our children. Operating from this Self Centered Awareness 'what's in for me' is the Second Noble Truth. Free from this is the Third Noble Truth. The way to freedom is the Fourth Noble Truth.

To understand **and** realise this wrong functioning, cycling in the 31 existences **and** to be free from it, is what Buddhism is all about. Whether the 31 existences are real or not, it does not matter; we take it as a Buddhist to learn and practise to be free from it.

We cannot do anything about the first kind of 'self'. We just live with it (maybe we will know when we are liberated). It is the 2nd kind of 'Self' that we need to deal with and the fourth Noble truth offers us the path to be free from this 'Self' – 'The Illusion of 'I'. We will understand more in Chapter 4, when we discuss the fourth Noble Truth.

The Four Noble Truths are an important principle in Buddhism, classically taught by the Buddha in the *Dharmacakra Pravartana Sūtra*. It provides the framework for understanding our human dilemma – Suffering and End of Suffering.

Chapter 1

SUFFERING- DUKKHA SACCA

The first Noble truth – "Suffering" *Dukkha*

"Life is like a box of chocolate, you do not know what you will get" a quote from the movie 'Forest Gump'. Life is full of mysteries. There are a lot of things we humans do not know. Typically we have more questions than answers. When we have more answers, they lead to more questions.

The Buddha said in the first Noble Truth – there is suffering.

We can classify human suffering into two groups. We need to understand them clearly, so that when we practice we know which is the one we need to emphasise on.

(1) Suffering caused by Nature – (Nature Condition) such as wild fire, flood, disease and so on, conditioned by the nature. When our ancestor(s) (human beings) inhibited the earth, Nature Conditions were there already. Our ancestor(s) had to face with these natural conditions and the creatures (animals – big ones) like dinosaurs. These are the suffering(s) caused by the natural conditions. Prince *Siddhatha* (Buddha to be) had to face with these natural conditions too, but his father tried to shield him from seeing them (old age, sickness

and death). Even after Enlightenment, the Buddha was not spared from the natural conditions. Buddha occasionally suffered (physically, not mentally) back pain and He passed away from diarrhea.

We do not have much control over these suffering(s). We can only do our best to alleviate them in whatever capacity we can.

(2) Suffering(s) caused by our own doings. Ignorance (not knowing) supported by greed, hatred and delusion, set up by our society, norms, traditions and so on.

There is a very good point by Elbert Einstein, showing that the world is in a mess. Doing the same thing will only get us the same results. The world we create at the level of thinking cannot be solved at the same level of thinking in which we created them.

Today the world is in a big mess. We mess with Nature, we try to manipulate Nature to satisfy our own greed. We are now suffering the dire consequences of our own actions. We are inside the mess of natural conditions and the man-made conditions. (See the book by Former Vice President Al Gore's New York Times #1 bestselling book and his video)

"Suffering is inevitable in our life but pain is optional". This is the normal philosophical understanding of suffering. Buddhism teaches us further about suffering. The Buddha stated that anyone who functions with greed, hatred, delusion (the defilements) the outcome is always additional suffering (pain) whether with good intentions or not. All our actions have consequences. The Great Dams that were once built to preserve water now cause floods at unprecedented level. We enjoy cars for ease of transportation at the increased cost of pollution. Nuclear energy turns to threats of world security. We no longer enjoy natural food but food that have been chemically processed and genetically altered affecting our overall health. Carbon footprint, climate change, pollution are some of the current issues indicating that we are not 'natural' anymore. Have we lost touch with 'Mother Nature'?

The Buddha further explained that unenlightened persons have greed, hatred and delusion as the unwholesome roots in the mind. So whatever the persons invented for the benefits of the people will finally end up in suffering. So this is why the world (or rather the Mother Nature) is now upset and out of control as if we are fast-forwarding to the end of the world. *We are going to die by our own hands!* So we can take that when we are ignorant, we add to tremendous suffering to others and ourselves.

We are caught up in the suffering so much that we do not understand ourselves anymore. We as human beings just simply function as a machine; we do not know who we really are (as human beings).

We do not know from where we come from and after dying we do not know where we are going to, what will happen to us after we die. Every Religion tries to explain the 'afterlife' according to their belief system, but there is no conclusive evidence. Christians say the deceased persons are waiting for the Judgment day (The Lord will decide according to their own good and bad deeds). But there is no conclusive proof. Buddhists explain that there are past lives, the present life and future lives and beings cycle in the 31 existences according to their *Kamma* – the good and bad deeds. If they do good, they will be reborn in happy existences, if they do bad they will be reborn in woeful states. Our goal is to be free from these 31 planes of existence. But if you look carefully, there is no conclusive evidence either. Every Religion explains about this unknowable field, but there is no conclusive proof.

If you carefully look at this unknowable field, there is no way to know about it, ***but to free from it is the best bet.*** Every Religion wants us to have a 'Faith' to this unknowable field. In Buddhism, we put our 'Faith' on the untold suffering in the 31 existences, so we practise to be liberated. This is where the 'Eightfold Path' comes in – The Fourth Noble Truth as expounded by the Buddha, the Path we need to *practice* in order to free from this 31 existences.

The Buddha expounded that this 31 planes of existences (cycling in the 31 existences) itself is 'Suffering'. So the moment we are born, we are inside the boat of suffering.

Some of the sufferings are suppressed in the mind's subconscious tendencies. They become scars, hidden desires and so forth. We become neurotic persons and have split or multiple personalities. We all (if not Liberated) behave like mad persons.

Since birth, we are already in a mess. We pick up the tendencies from our parents and fellow human beings which are greed, hatred, jealously and so on and all the other conditions set up by the norms, society. We function like a machine, constantly calculating what's in for me as we live in the world. We are run by our defilements and conditions. This corrupted consciousness leads us by the nose, which is so fast and automatic. That is why the Buddha stated that mind is the forerunner of all things. Aging, disease, death, become our pattern, our blue print, life after life. Actually we are not supposed to be like this. See "Ageless Body, Timeless Mind" by Dr. Deepak Chopra.

From the time we are born till the time we die, we have to face sorrow, lamentation, pain, distress and despair, association with what is not loved; separation from what is loved, not getting what we want, getting what we do not want plus all the mind afflictions. We all suffer in this same manner, no exceptions. We are inside the same boat and the boat is sinking very fast. There are only very few people who are awake and free from this boat. We need to be free from this boat. To be free is what Buddhism all about - Suffering and end of suffering.

The first Noble Truth is explained as follows: -

("This is the noble truth of suffering: <u>birth</u> is suffering, <u>aging</u> is suffering, <u>illness</u> is suffering, <u>death</u> is suffering; sorrow, lamentation, pain, grief and despair are suffering; union with what is displeasing is suffering; separation from what is pleasing is suffering; not to get what one wants is suffering; in brief, the <u>five aggregates</u> subject to <u>clinging</u> are suffering)

It means that birth and death and everything in between are suffering. Five aggregates are: - Body (material organs, eye, ear, nose and so on), Feelings, Perception (memory), Mental Formations and Consciousness. When we (the consciousness) perceive the objects through our six senses, the roots of greed, hatred and delusion are already in our mental formation. Wrong view leads to wrong intentions and wrong intentions lead to wrong speech and actions. We end up in suffering and more suffering.

Let's look into more details. Before our first ancestor(s) got into this earth, there were already existence of other beings, plants and animals. With the chemical changes, cells began to change and divide, combine and so on. The life forms and the material things they were inhibiting infringe upon each other, influencing each other. When the first human being(s), our ancestors got here, they were already inside this conditioned state. In other words they were already in the suffering state. From then and until today, we are inside the suffering state starting from our ancestor(s).

If you look further you will see that our so-called 'Earth', the world is a tiny little planet in the whole solar system and the universe. The planets in the solar system are always changing. The universe come into existence and disappear, never constant – they die when the conditions to exist are no longer there. The planets and the universe are *Anicca* (not permanent), *Dukkha* (suffering - whatever is not permanent is suffering) and *Anatta* (no controlling factor). If we hold on to something for our happiness, when it changes then we suffer.

Everything is in a flux, constantly changing moment by moment. Nothing stays constant for even one moment. Everything arises and passes away. What then is birth and death? Seeing the true nature of phenomena, you will have no problem in dying (and birth). You will know how to live (fully) and die peacefully. No problem in life!

Who is responsible for this? Who put human being(s), our first ancestor(s) into this suffering state?

There is no way to find out with our limited and distorted mind. These are unknowable fields, but when one's consciousness is clean and pure – depending upon one's transformation of consciousness, one starts to see and understand the hidden – unknowable fields.

We all want to be free from these conditioned states of suffering to one that is completely free. The Buddha stated that there is the unborn, the unconditioned, the uncreated, the un-fabricated, which is *Nibbana*.

There is a teaching of the Buddha that if we are shot by an arrow, we are not interested to find out who shot the arrow, what the arrow make of and so forth; we are more concerned to heal the pain. The Buddha is only concerned about suffering and end of suffering.

The first Noble Truth states that there is suffering. This suffering must be fully understood. Sayalay Susila from Malaysia, says it beautifully like this - "Unless we know and see *Dukkha* (suffering), we have little reason to practice. When we truly understand *Dukkha*, it puts our practice immediately back on track".

Bottom line we understand that the Buddha's teaching separates the suffering that we experience because of the way life apparently is from the suffering that is created emotionally from not wanting things to be the way it is. When we understand this, we are able to let go of the holding on. We understand the nature of phenomena in the things, the people, the world, and the universe and not attached to them. This is the main theme of Buddhist Meditation.

Note: - Please see my book Buddhism and Liberation, how these defilements and conditions got into our mind.

Chapter 2

THE CAUSE OF SUFFERING
– SAMUDAYA SACCA

The cause of suffering can then be deduced to two important factors:

(1) Greed, hatred and delusion and the conditions supporting them

(2) The mental process – Wrong thought process (Wrong View)

How do the defilements and conditions arise in our mind?

To understand this we need to understand the five aggregates (*upādānakkhandha*). The Buddha pointed out that this illusion of "I" is nothing but the five aggregates. There is a body that comprises of the four elements (earth, water, fire and wind). And then there is a mind that makes up of feelings, perceptions, mental formations and consciousness. This consciousness is accompanied by different kinds of mental factors that allow us to act in ways that are skillful and ways that are unskillful. These five aggregates, the Buddha summed up as what constitute all the physical and mental phenomena of existence. They function together when a person perceives any of the six sense objects (sight, sound, smell, taste, tactile objects and thoughts).

(1) **Corporeality group *(rūpa-kkhandha)*:** This is the 'material form' that the senses pass through - eye, ear, nose, tongue

and body. The material aggregates, together with the mind perceive the objects. This material form by itself does not know the object. So together with the mind, the Buddha explained that there are six senses.

(2) **Consciousness group** *(viññāna-kkhandha):* We need consciousness to cognize any objects. Without consciousness, there can be no mental factors as they coexist. Hence one cannot perceive or function when consciousness is not there.

(3) **Perception** *(saññā):* This aggregate perceives or recognizes both the physical and mental objects through its contact with the senses. Perception helps us to remember and recognize distinctions of one object from another. This distinction makes us familiar with the object or idea when we sense it in the future. So perception is memory; we recognize this is Jack, this is a table and so on.

(4) **Feelings** *(vedanā):* - This aggregate of feeling or sensation can be either pleasant, unpleasant or neutral and they arise from contact. When seeing or hearing occurs, it creates an idea or thought and we get a feeling about that idea or thought. When feeling changes, the physical body also changes – like if you are angry, the face become red and so on. It lives on with dualities, like love and hate. Like and dislike and so on. Note: - Feeling has a special place in our practice. The Buddha wants us to watch this feeling as *ANICCA* – Impermanent. Because it is impermanent and it changes, we suffer *DUKKHA* when we are attached to something. An arising feeling cannot be prevented – no controlling factor(s) – *ANATTĀ*. We practise to experience directly that feeling is *Anicca, Dukkha* and *Anattā*. <u>**So 'feeling' can be a source of our craving or it can be a gateway to liberation.**</u>

Feeling is a natural state and not a problem. Only when we are attached to the feeling "If only I have this or that I will be happy" does suffering arise. Money is not a problem, having more money is not a problem. Only when we are overly attached to the money, holding on to it obsessively then suffering arises. Learning is not a problem, only when we become proud because we are learned is the problem. So that "holding on" the object is the real problem.

Feelings are not reliable. They change over time. This is the way it is. So the more you are attached to your feelings, the more you suffer.

The Liberated persons only have the universal feeling which is Loving – Kindness, Compassion, Altruistic joy and Equanimity – they are unconditional, no "buts" or "if only" or any conditions for its abundance.

This 'Feeling(s)' is a cross road for craving or wisdom to arise. When we are not mindful, defilements easily creep in. But when we can see feeling as feeling, we are able to sense that the object is one thing and the sensation is another. This separation is important as it provides the space for wisdom (seeing the things as they truly are) to arise where the mental energy is not clouded to the physical data (in the memory).

Feeling(s) combined with attachment manifests in different forms. We can have angry feeling, happy feeling, romantic feeling, guilty feeling and so on. These different moods come about when there is reactivity of the mind. We want things to be what we want and not what they actually are.

It is challenging to tell the mind to stay focus on one object. We abuse our mind so much, we pamper the mind so much so that the mind cannot be left alone – it needs object(s) to dwell on. We 'day dream', we stay in thinking or in our dreams (actually dreaming is an activity of the mind – playing, thinking sub-consciously). That is why we are exhausted all the time, thinking about the past and planning for the future (with attachment / desire) that we need longer rest. Buddha and all the liberated persons do not need so much rest; they rest for a while only.

More than that, the mind needs stimulation, entertainment, gossip and so on. When bored, it finds something to do, turning on the TV or getting something to eat. It is endlessly searching for external stimuli to satisfy its senses. It is always looking for something more, something stronger. This is "wanting to want", a disease our culture keeps nourishing.

More than that, the mind keeps computing, calculating so much that it becomes a habit pattern. It is hard wired into our biology as part of what helps us survive. Our lives seem to revolve around desire for ever-new experiences, even as we see how fleeting they are. The difficulty of escaping the gravitational field of the world of sense pleasures conditions us into the habit of accumulation or we call addictions. This wanting mind, the feeling that we never have enough, is very strong. It takes us for a ride, a long ride that you are no longer yourself anymore, you become the objects.

The wonderful paradox of the spiritual path is that transitory phenomena as objects of our desire leave us feeling unsatisfied, while as objects of mindfulness they can become vehicles of awakening. All defilements arise because of wrong view that leads to wrong thoughts, thinking, calculating "what's in for me" in all our endeavors. When we pay attention to the present moment, we can follow the links of how we get caught in desire – sensing, contact, feeling, desire, grasping and so on. When we pay close attention, we can break the connection between feelings and desire. We can observe the conditioning of contact, noting the feeling of pleasantness and then

11

stay mindful of that feeling. The defilements and conditions never come in.

If we are not liberated, the greed, hatred, pride and so on (the defilements, plus the conditions) turn the person into an Ego-entity, Personality (*attā*), 'Big Ego' or 'For me'. Because of these, human beings abuse 'Mother Nature', take advantage of each other and now we can see how suffering originates.

'Ego-entity, Personality (*Attā*) pushes (volitional acts - *Kamma*) you into the next existence (*Attā* wants to be immortal. The *'Unfinished Data'* – in the 'Latent fields - tendencies' (*Anusaya*) (they are in the form of feelings - with attachments *tanhā*, strong clinging *upādānam*), will carry on to next existence as *Kammic* energy force.

(5) **Mental-Formation (*sankhāra*):** This is where the beauty of Buddhism shows up. From up there the 4 aggregates we collect the data (physically and psychological) and from here the mind is formed, deciding how to act *and* re-act. If we are not enlightened the attachment from the 'Feelings' (the 'For Me') takes over and the reactivity (very fast and automatic) is always unskillful. We have no consideration for others, we do not care about 'Mother Nature' and in the end all these lead to suffering. Because of ignorance, the clinging to becoming or not becoming, we make contracts for the next existence. This is what Buddha called '*Samsara* – Rounds of Rebirth, Perpetual Wandering'.

Let me give you an example; -

You know U Khema Wuntha; you got the physical data of U Khema. When you meet U Khema, the consciousness group (*viññāna kkhandha*) perceives through your corporeality group (*rūpa-kkhandha*) eye, ear nose and so on – the senses, compare with the physical data in your memory (*saññā*) and you recognize that this is U Khema. In the mean time the feeling(s) (*vedanā*) rolls it up and the mental formation (*sankhāra*) decides how to react (function). It depends on how much your attachment to the feeling(s) you have towards U Khema, the more attachments, the more craving, and the more clinging – to U Khema.

Through love, hate, like and dislike (attachment) towards the objects, we compare, judge and compute. This is how we function in this world clinging towards the object, clinging to an idea. Mental formations work precisely in this way leading to suffering. Even with good intention(s) (if you have attachments) as time goes by we suffer.

Let us continue to study more on these five aggregates.

Buddha pointed out as "What is called individual existence is in reality nothing but a mere process of those mental and physical phenomena". Inside these 5 aggregates there is no self-dependent, real Ego-entity or Personality (*attā*), simply no "Big EGO" or "For Me".

The mind should be 'as it is'; simply the mind and body (the 5 aggregates), no sub consciousness or super consciousness. 'No Big Ego' or 'No Small Ego', No 'For Me'. We simply function as 5 aggregates (with the universal understanding of Love and Kindness, Compassion, Altruistic Joy and Equanimity)

Can we balance these defilements and conditions by doings good deeds? Can we do 'mambo jumbo' to get rid of them? Can somebody get rid of them for us, with super natural powers?

In dept understanding of 'Feeling(s)

Feeling plays an important role in *'Paticcasamuppāda'* 'Dependent Origination' – doctrine of the conditionality of all physical and psychical phenomena, as taught by the Buddha.

Phassa-paccayā vedanā; 'Contact conditions 'Feelings'.

Vedanā-paccayā tanhā; 'Feelings condition craving'.

Tanhā-paccayā upādāna; 'Craving conditions clinging.'

Let us understand in plain English about the feelings: -

(1) When you make a 'Contact' (with object(s), 'Feeling' comes up.

(2) 'Feelings' (if not careful - mostly we do not careful) will lead you to 'Craving'.

(3) 'Craving' will lead you to 'Clinging'.

The stronger the clinging (to objects, feeling, emotions) the stronger our urge to act out unskillfully and the end result is always suffering.

This clinging to 'Life' is what propels us in the 'Round of Rebirth, Perpetual Wandering' – *Samsara.(being reborn and die in the 31 existences)*

Note: - Intention is volition. All volitional acts (doing as attachment) create *kamma.* Even when one is doing meritorious deeds, if one is not careful, one clings to the merits and hence we can say that they have already made a contract for the next existence (doing meritorious deeds for the next good life). This is in opposite to the path of liberation. They continue to buy insurances life after life.

Very unfortunately Buddhism is like business these days – Buddhist monks, nuns and other religious leaders acting out as the sellers, the devotees are the enthusiastic buyers and the commodity is the meritorious deeds (for next good existence). The places of trading are the temples and monasteries, occasionally in the devotee's house when invited. The motto is always "Do good, get good." Consciously or unconsciously the devotees have certain expectations or rewards for their good actions. This is business, spiritual trading. Offering a plate of fruits and expecting to be born in heaven!

Please do not get me wrong; nowadays the conducting of religious ceremonies itself is very much like buying and selling. Fortunately not all monasteries - not all monks (and nuns) are like that.

Here we must clearly understand the difference between natural or ordinary feeling(s) and the attachment that arises from feeling(s). There is nothing wrong with the natural feeling(s) (conditions) like eating habits because of the country we are bought up, mental habits of our races, countries and so on, but the deep attachment to the habit reinforces the 'entity – I, me or mine', clinging, the holding on to the feeling(s). The illusion of "I", the big 'Ego', the 'I', everything 'For me' *(Atta)* is the real problem.

Let me make this clearer, the enlightened person who is brought up with fish paste will still have the liking for the fish paste when he sees it and takes it, but he does not have any attachment to fish paste. If there is fish paste, that's fine. If there is no fish paste, there's no problem either. Likewise the enlightened person who is brought up with cheese and butter also never has problem with the cheese and butter. The problem is the attachment to the fish paste, cheese and butter.

Again: - stay with me, open your mind and follow me and see: - The attachment *(tanhā)* (to objects) usually ends up in clinging, leads to strong clinging *(upādāna)* (to things, people and *life itself – obviously or sub consciously. This is why Buddhists when doing the rituals and performing the ceremonies is like buying insurance for the next life.* As long as you hold on to this, the 'Round of Rebirth, Perpetual Wandering' – *Samsara* becomes reality itself and you are caught inside. The illusion of 'I' (you) **created** the 31 existences and you are caught up inside it. Only very - very few realize it and are awake. They are the 'Awakened Ones'.

Sottāpanna – 'Stream-Winner' – entering the stream of Liberation (the first stage) one has no attachment to rites and ritual. Together with no more 'big EGO', no skeptical doubt – he knows the way to Liberation.

Mogoke Sayādaw, The eminent meditation master from Burma use this *'Paticcasamuppāda'* 'Dependent Origination' stating that the 'Ignorance and Craving (*Tanhā*) are the main causes for the 'Round of Rebirth, Perpetual Wandering' – *Samsara*. Using his famous chart, he wants us to penetrate and see how we are constantly being caught up and how to be free contemplating at the point of Feeling before it turns into Craving, into Clinging and Becoming.

In *Vippassa* meditation we train our mind to look at contact. Right there, we can choose to act or not to act. When there is pleasant feeling, our default is attachment and when there is unpleasant feeling aversion. We can direct and terminate craving right there. Feeling is *"ANICCA"* – Impermanent. Because it is impermanent and changing, we suffer *"DUKKHA"*. We do not have absolute control over our feelings – no controlling factor(s) – *"ANATTA"*. *Vipassana meditation* helps us to recognize this link between feeling and craving. It is the easiest to break because here the craving is conscious. So we can witness and understand the pull, the urge to act and choose not to act. We can see the unfolding of impermanence, instability and non-self right there.

In simple understanding using the simple words will be as follows: -

When we are happy, we laugh; when we are sad, we cry. These are moods or attachments to the feelings. The more you are attached to the object(s) – material things or beings, the more you will cling and depend on them and the stronger the sensation. The nature of the objects or experience is impermanence. If you are attached to them and want them to be what you desire, so when they change, you suffer. 'Understanding' is wisdom; failure to recognize this is 'Ignorance' (not knowing). Ignorance and craving is always accompanied by Greed, Hatred and Delusion, the 3 'Roots – *'biologically Rooted"* – in human beings (24 Conditioned Relationship – *Paticcasamuppāda* – doctrine of the conditionality of all physical and mental phenomena).

When there is ignorance, we are not able to see "feeling in the feeling." Much of the time we are in contact with our perceptions because they create images in accordance with desire and they can trigger such powerful volition that we become carried away. When we are able to recognize Tanha (craving) in its fully conscious form, we can then know its deceptivity. When we understand that "Feelings" are not real, we no longer believe in them. Naturally, the mind quiets down and letting go of the holding on is possible.

With this proper guidance – understanding – the whole map and understanding of the 'Nature of Liberation, we can practice correctly for Liberation. Then we are operating out of understanding rather than ignorance.

Chapter 3

THE END OF SUFFERING - NIRODHA SACCA

There is suffering. There is a cause for suffering. If the Buddha stopped there, then our practice will be futile. The Buddha went further to assure us that there is an end to suffering and showed us the path that will lead to end of suffering. So the Buddha is concerned about suffering and end of suffering. Speculations about the past, who is responsible for our suffering is not important, ending suffering is what matters to the Buddha.

There is nothing wrong with the objects and people outside us. They happen when the right cause and conditions are there. This is 'Nature'. They are neither good nor bad (in a psychological sense). They are just as "what is" at the present moment. Suffering is not outside us; it is all happening inside us. Because we cannot accept and acknowledge, "what is" we try to manipulate the situation according to our desires or aversion. Our mind fabricates all sorts of things, doing everything except surrendering to the unconditional acceptance of the present moment.

Example: - When we see a diamond and if we are not mindful, greed arises. We no longer see "what is" but rather "if only I have the diamond." This fabrication of mind, if not checked or recognized will lead to manifestation of unskillful actions (stealing, robbing). Maybe you like the diamond but cannot afford it. So envy, jealousy or aversion arise. The problem is not the diamond; the problem is our attachment to the diamond. So our practice is to recognize the attachment and see it's impermanent nature so that we no longer have to act out in ignorance. When a liberated one sees the diamond, they see just the diamond (minus the greed). The problem is never outside us; the problem is always inside us.

Note: - When we practise *Vipassana* (Insight – understanding) Meditation, we do not say 'This body is suffering' or 'Suffering arises because we got this body'. There is nothing wrong with the body, it changes when the condition(s) changes. Actually it is in your mind that you are un-satisfied with the body, thinking that the body makes you suffer. Of course there is physical suffering (pain when we sit long in one posture) but it is in the mind that suffering arises. Pain and suffering are two different stages. Pain is rather a kind of nature and suffering is you built up from the pain. When you understand the true nature of the body (and mind) you can still feel the pain, but no suffering. We practise to be free from the defilements inside the mind, not pushing away, denying or attached to the things and people. This fact is very important when we practise according to the Fourth Noble Truth, coming up in the next chapter.

We are so conditioned since we are born (started from our ancestors) in the world. We are conditioned by the places we live and experience, by our parents, culture, education, media and in turn we condition each other and the environment.

So how does this conditioning take place?

(1) The mind knows only how to function in the mundane world; the mind only *dwells* in the world by comparing and contrasting with the known data (from the memory). We

are programmed to operate like this and like that because we think that this is the only way we can be happy.

(2) When the illusion of 'I' develops, it functions as 'For Me' state only.

Note: - The illusion of "I" started from our first ancestor(s), handed down by our parents, generation by generation. White people, black people, Asian all alike, function with this "For Me" state. (Please see my book 'Buddhism and Liberation)

The older we get, the more experienced and automatic we are in this conditioning process. It becomes our reality. We just operate like an autopilot. We desire for sensual pleasures even though we know they do not last. When one desire subsides, craving for the next one begins. This conditioning, this chronic state of dissatisfaction continues to heighten as our modus operandi.

We are trapped in this web of conditioning – searching but not finding in *'Samsara'* – 'Round of Rebirth'. The mind is caught up in 'Time', 'Space' and 'Causation'.

"Time" – Psychological Time *(holding/ longing to past and future)*, the mind can only understand and function in the time frame – of 31 existences. It cannot understand beyond this time frame. We hold on to this 31 existences as something that happened in the past, something that will happen in the future and something that is happening in the present moment. That is why the unenlightened ones continue to cycle in the rounds of rebirth. *(31 Existence itself is in the 'Time Mode', in the Past, in the present life (you are now), and will be in the future (in 31 existence).* They could not break free from this time frame and see the possibility of Liberation, which is timeless *(akaliko)*. In meditation we try and break down this time frame by paying attention to what is happening in the here and now (*Timeless*), and touching the taste of Freedom.

"Space" – Mind can only function (psychologically) by comparing, with reference to our perception. This duality of mind, the good and bad, love and hate, this method and that method are dependent on external conditions and stimuli. This makes us separate from others. But when we begin to see the interconnectedness between all things, ourselves and others, we come to a space where we can experience inner joy by just "simply being."

"Causation" – Unenlightened Ones live in the world of reasoning. Since young, we are trained to think as 'for me'. No matter what's the problem, we think for ourselves out of it.

"Love versus Attachment. Attachment is the very opposite of Love" Jetsunma Tenzin Palmo

Love says "I want you to be happy." Attachment says "I want you to make me happy."

We (unenlightened ones) live in the Attachment states. We live in dualities - give and take, always calculating what is in it for me. In meditation we try to recognize this limited functioning and let the mind break free as it goes though 'Transformation of Consciousness'.

Actually these Time, Space and Causation refer to the '*Kamma*' as mentioned in Buddhism, which makes cycling in 31 existences - '*Samsara* – Round of Rebirth, Perpetual Wandering'.

Our mind cannot understand the Liberation state, because it is stuck up in the worldly things, just like a frog in the well cannot perceive the outside of the well.

There is only one mind but different kinds of consciousness depending on the mental factors. The mind function as consciousness (5 aggregates) manifest as feelings. It function as 'thought process'. So we can largely classify the mind under two categories (of consciousness)

1. The Original Mind (when function - alive and conscious and perceiving, it can refers as consciousness), which is pure, unconditioned and unlimited, uncreated, unmoved but they are not permanent also. They come up spontaneously when the right causes and conditions are there. (One mind as original consciousness)

2. The Corrupted Mind (when function - alive and conscious and perceiving, it can refers as consciousness) which is clouded, fabricated, created, constantly moving and never satisfied. (***Same One*** *mind* function as corrupted consciousness)

    There is only one mind. Mind is mind, it is neither good or bad, it is just to know the object and function. But when it function as consciousness and it become as good or bad, skillful or unskillful. We are stuck up in this corrupted mind - consciousness.

As long as we live, our mind is an inseparable part of us. As a result, we are always up and down, governed by our moods. We need to see through this veil in order to see what is clear, clean and cool – the Original Mind which is always with us. It has never left us.

The 2nd Noble Truth explains the cause of suffering. The 3rd Noble Truth explains the cessation of the cause of suffering. We recognize the Corrupted Consciousness and everything it fabricates so that we can be awake to the Original Mind - Consciousness.

Which is more important? Do you want to be happy or do you want to be free? Until we are serious about liberation, until we make our practice a priority in our lives, we are not ready enough to perceive the Liberation state. The Fourth Noble Truth – The Eightfold Noble Path provides the complete path to train our body and mind to a state where we can understand and appreciate (*Anumāna* – guessing the *Nibbana*) getting the taste of freedom – Liberation. We then walk along, adapting (*Anuloma*) till the Liberation state.

Every Religious Leader tries to point out the Liberation state in his own ways and define what liberation is all about.

There are unknowable fields in our human life. We are only exposed to what happen to us in this very life. Before we were born and after we die, these areas are unknowable fields. Every Religion tries to provide an explanation, ***but there is no conclusive proof.*** Even as we are living there are many mysteries that we are not able to understand. Why does one grow old, become sick and die?

Buddhism explains these - before birth and after death, as cycling in 31 existences - '*Samsara* – Round of Rebirth, Perpetual Wandering'. ***But there is no conclusive proof*** (our mind is very limited to know for sure). We learn about the 31 existences, the tremendous suffering that we have gone through. The Buddha said that our tears collected are more than the collective waters from the four great oceans. We dread having to go through more suffering in future. ***We just need to be free from it. These unknowable fields are not important; the important thing is to realize the suffering and end of suffering. Nobody can free us; we have to do the practice ourselves.***

The Buddha said that attachment is the cause of all our suffering as in the 2nd Noble Truth. So our practice is to find a way to break the link; attachments have to be abandoned. The psychological links, longings, anxieties, and expectations – all these have to be broken.

Ultimately we have to recognize the fear and insecurity and come out from there. *The mind is what it is, neither weak nor strong, neither a master nor a slave. The mind job is just to function. It is neither good nor bad.*

When there is no object, there is no mind. Mind comes up when there is an object. The body is also combination of cells. Then who are you? Isn't it a very interesting issue?

Please see my book, Buddhism and Liberation to understand the nature of freedom.

This is the Third Noble Truth that the Buddha that pointed out.

Let us understand in more detail.

Now we know that the psychological Links, the attachments are part and parcel of us, run by the illusion of 'I', which is handed down by our ancestor(s), and we develop it along our childhood and manhood and we are handing down to our children. Our children will hand down to their children. When and how are we going to be free from these attachments? This is what 'Four Noble Truths' is all about.

We need to eradicate the wrong thought process by the five aggregates - cause of the suffering. (We need to be free from the Illusion of 'I')

Now it is very obvious that the Illusion of 'I' attaches and stays in the worldly things. Our mind knows only how to function in the worldly area; the mind needs worldly object(s) to hang on to, that is, the mind has to have some kind of sensual desire (for me), to stimulate the mind etc. They do not understand the nature of freedom (from worldly life). Only when you can start un-holding the attachments (to the worldly things), you start to get the glimpse of Liberation.

Does your practice lead to non-attachment (to the worldly things) or just simply doing as a part of the routine daily activities? Buddha pointed out that we must eradicate the attachments to the world (*Nirodha*). This is the 3rd. Noble Truth.

So how are we going to be free? How can we cut the links, the attachments to the world? We can do so in the following ways.

(1) Urgency, an overwhelming desire (to Liberate)

You need to have the strong, passionate desire to Liberate. We need to have the sparks – to liberate, that is why we meditate. But do you hold on to the sparks and develop them into flame, or let it turn into routine matter? Does it have 'Predominance' – *Adhipati* effect in the mind? (Taught by the Buddha in 24 Conditional Relationship – *Adhipati Paccaya, the third one*)

We can reflect the life story of the Buddha. The Buddha to be, Prince *Siddhattha Gotama*– had this sense of calling, the challenge to be free is so overwhelming, the desire to be free is so intense, and it becomes a passion (*chanda*).

When he encountered an old man, sick man, a dead man and finally a recluse – who had gone forth from the household life and put on the bark-dyed clothes, immediately this had a strong impact in his mind that propelled him to search for an answer, to find an end to all sufferings. These four heavenly sights are not reserved for Prince Siddhartha alone. We have seen them hundreds of times too. The question is whether they shake us up from our sleep as Prince Siddhartha did.

That urgency is what matters, that immediacy to find out why we suffer and how to end our suffering.

(When *Channa*, the royal servant and head charioteer of *Siddhattha explained about the four signs, Siddhattha's* desire was so great that it had a strong influence in his mind. The Prince was in the 3rd. condition *adhipati* – Predominance, a condition from the 24 conditional relationships. More over it was the first and heavy predominance - preponderance *'Chanda'* – concentrated intention in the mind, which is dependent upon the mental phenomena associated with them. When this kind of status influences the mind, it is very hard to break away, it dominates the consciousness (mind) and it will investigate all the way through, up to Liberation.

Do we have this kind of obsession/passion in our practice?

(2) Dispassionate with the worldly things.

The Buddha said that the 1st Noble Truth has to be understood. We need to come to terms with *Dukkha*, that doing what we are doing does not lead us any closer to real happiness. We begin to realize that there is a higher happiness that the Buddha was talking about. This happiness is not born out of attachment, of having more. It is the relinquishment of attachment, non-clinging, not holding on to any attachment.

There is a story of *'Patacara'*, a woman during Buddha's time, who lost everyone dear to her in a short period of time (her husband and two sons). Overcome with grief, she walked around town barely covered in a cloak, and thus became known as cloak walker, or *"Patacara."* The Buddha give a profound teaching to her about life. Alas she came to a realization that it is impossible that death would not occur. Her mind is settled, no more grief, no more anger - to life, That moment she understood, her attachments and grief were relinquished through understanding the nature of impermanence (right view). This wisdom (understanding) release all the attachments - the holdings as 'mine, 'for me'.

All of the 'Theragatha - Verses of the Elder Monks") and "Therigatha - Verses of the Elder Nuns" are about Liberation and the relinquishment of attachment. *We cannot have liberation with attachment.*

Do you have this kind of seeing about your life in your practice? Do you have a strong reason to drop these attachment like a hot potato?

See Tipitaka » Sutta Pitaka » Khuddaka Nikaya » Context of the Therigatha - Therigatha

Verses of the Elder Nuns and a short play of Patacara in 'You Tube' by the local artists.

(3) The mind is in the Here and Now.

Can you train the mind to be in present moment? Without wandering, thinking, expecting anything as you meditate? If you can get to that moment of 'staying with the present moment' (quiet, serene), then at that moment only, you can touch of the nature of freedom (a taste of freedom) – and carry on to release all the attachments to the worldly things. The minute you are aware that the mind wanders, thinks or expects, at that moment you are already in the here and now.

Being mindful is not difficult, the difficulty is to remember to be mindful.

See the example of Sun Lun Sayadaw – a famous meditation master of Burma. He was illiterate. He was a farmer who practiced to let his mind stay in the present moment. When he was plowing, his mind was in the plowing. When he cut the grass for his cows, his mind was in the present moment and so on. Suddenly (when his mind was in the present moment), he noticed that people were running around with greed, hatred and delusion – and they were all suffering. He just dropped his plowing things and ran to the village monastery and became a monk. Later on, many learned monks tested his knowledge on *Dhamma*. He could answer them very well, not through book knowledge but through his direct experience. Although he did not have any education, he saw the truth, and he realized the 3rd Noble Truth.

Can you get the mind to be in the here and now? Are you practicing like this to get the mind to be in the present moment?

In this era I believe 'Eckhart Tolle' is the best teacher pointing out the 'present moment'.

You can find the biography of Sun Lun Sayadaw from the Internet – The detailed biography of The Venerable Sun Lun Gu Kyaung Sayadaw U Kavi of Myingyan.

Actually this is the main method Buddha gave us to quiet the mind – to be in the present moment. He taught us the *Ānāpāna Sati* – Mindfulness of breathing and instructed us on the *Mahā-Satipatthā Sutta* to understand the true nature of our body and mind. *Vipassanā* method (***as a technique and method***) comes later, much - much later, in the 20th century, starting in Burma. All the famous *Vipassana* meditation masters started in Burma and in the 20th century.

(Please see my book 'Buddhism and Liberation)

(4) Understanding Things As They Are.

Can you train the mind to understand the true nature of body and mind – and let go of any holding (psychologically) to the body and mind?

Vipassana meditation teaches us to see the nature of phenomena especially our body and mind. This is the goal of Vipassana, clear seeing.

Are you really practicing to see the true nature of the things?

Do you really see the true nature of the things?

Most of us are confused with 'Vipassanā meditation' and the 'present moment' I mentioned above.

If you look carefully at the above facts, you will find that all of them refer to dropping the holding on – the attachments.

There must be a strong encounter to drop the attachment, dispassion towards attachment. There must be a reason, the right view (wisdom), and the genuine interest and curiosity to go to the further shore (the transcendental world).

Is your practice building up this kind of strong encounter? We must be like spiritual warriors, otherwise it is unlikely that we can abandon the attachments.

Chapter 4

THE PATH LEADING TO THE CESSATION OF SUFFERING: (DUKKHA NIRODHA GĀMINĪ PAṬIPADĀ MAGGA)

This is the noble truth of the way leading to the cessation of suffering - the Noble Eightfold Path: Right View, Right Thought, Right Speech, Right Action, Right Livelihood, Right Effort, Right Mindfulness and Right Concentration.

The Four Noble Truths teaches us about suffering, the cause of suffering, the cessation of suffering and the way to end suffering. The fourth Noble Truth is non other than 'The Eightfold Path'.

The Eightfold Path:-

(1) We need to clearly understand that even though it says as 'Path', the Path is not a road to walk on. It is not like an end of the road where we will reach *Nibbana* – Liberation is'. *Nibbana* is not the result of anything, not something that is 'man-made'. It is not as a reward after the Path. If you look at the eightfold path, it is to be practiced, not as a road literally to walk along. That is why it can be referred to as 'Pathless Path'. Please see my book 'Pathless Path to Liberation'.

(2) This eightfold path is for us to practice and cultivate. It is not a step-by-step menu that we practise linearly. It is a holistic blueprint for practice. It is a complete path where we practise all the factors and not pick and choose. These eight factors support one another. When we practise one factor, the other seven factors are there.

(3) We practise to understand the nature of the body and mind that they are *Anicca* – impermanent, *Dukkha* – Suffering and *Anatta* – no controlling factors. Can we ask our body not to age, sick or die? Truly we do not own this body or mind, we cannot control it. See this clearly; we can release the psychological holding – clinging to the body.

Moreover, as I pointed out before, we are supposed to clear the *Kamma* condition. The natural condition, we cannot do much, only we can take care of our body and mind. After we are enlightened, we live under the natural condition(s) and when the time comes (to die) we leave the body and mind and there is no cycling back in the 31 existences.

(4) If we want to practice seriously, we must keep aside the 31 existences from the mind. There must be no longing for good existences or fear to fall down to lower existences. Any psychological link to the 31 existences, such as longing for the good existences or the fear to be reborn in woeful states has to be cleared from the mind. It is *Kamma* that fuels the energy for the continued rebirths. *Kamma* is the resultant of the Illusion of "I", *ATTA*. This fear and insecurity of future births is what gravitates us in the 31 existences. We must never let the thought of rebirth in the 31 existences influence our meditation. (You will understand the true nature of the 31 existences later on). (Please see my book "Buddhism and Liberation" about the 31 existence).

First we need to tame the mind to be soft and gentle. We need to quiet the mind ***naturally***. If this is not done naturally, even though the mind is quiet, it is still man-made state as there is volition to quiet, to direct the mind to quiet.

Generally there are three basic parts we need to be aware. Recognising them makes our practice easy to follow.

(1) Taming the mind (relax and soften the mind) - *Sila*

(Right Speech – *Sammā-vācā,* Right Action – *Sammā-Kammanta-,* Right Livelihood – *Sammā-Ājīva*)

(1) Quiet the mind – *Samadhi*

(Right Effort – *Sammā-Vāyāma,* Right Mindfulness – *Sammā-Sati,* Right Concentration - *Sammā-Samādhi*)

(2) Understanding the true nature of things - *Panna*

Wisdom (Understanding) – Right View or Right Understanding – *Sammā-Diṭṭhi,* Right Thought – *Sammā Sankappa*)

The path is:- *Sila* – Morality, *Samadhi* – Concentration and *Panna* – Wisdom.

Bhikkhu Bodhi explains "with a certain degree of progress all eight factors can be present simultaneously, each supporting the others. However, until that point is reached, some sequence in the unfolding of the path is inevitable.

It means that when we are practicing on a morality level we *emphasize* as taming the mind, taking the precepts, accumulating the meritorious deeds and so on. When we are ready to meditate, we concentrate to quiet the mind and so on. When one is stable on the path, these eightfold path presents simultaneously, supporting each other, hand in hand as we practice.

This is the way to practice the Noble Eightfold Path.

We tame our mind, we let the mind be quiet (naturally) and we develop right view. We experience directly the body and mind and their intrinsic nature *(annica, dukkha and anatta)*. This 'Right Understanding' will lead to the release of the holding (attachments) to the worldly things.

This 'Right View' will pave and tread the way to Liberation. There are landmarks along the way. Repeatedly we *understand* the 1st Noble Truth, *abandon* the 2nd Noble Truth. Abandonment of craving (2nd Noble Truth) is the cause for cessation of suffering, the 3rd Noble Truth which must be *realized*. If there are strange things that we encounter in the journey, small to big super natural powers, we can acknowledge them but do not attach to them. Practising like this will lead to wisdom, understanding the things as they truly are.

Note: - In this Eightfold Path, there is no saying about the *Samatha*-Tranquility or *Vipassanā* - Insight method. It just simply says to tame the mind and let the mind be quiet naturally and understand the nature of the things. We need both concentration and insight; they complement each other like the wings of a bird to reach the further shore.

Let me give you as an example: -

> The diamond – we see, we understand the true nature of a diamond and we realize that the diamond makes human beings crazy. People die because of the diamond. If you really understand

the true nature of the diamond, you can release the craving and free yourself of the diamond. This is the way of *Vipassanā* Method – understanding the true nature (of the diamond). Likewise if you understand the true nature of the body (and mind), that they are ever changing and we cannot control the body (and mind) it goes on to ageing, prone to disease and so on. When we understand the true nature of the body, we are not going to hate the body nor love the body. We understand the body (and mind) is subjected to old age, disease and death; we can release the psychological holding – craving to the body and mind and to free them. This is *Vipassanā* Method.

Greed inside us makes us crazy about the diamond, not that the diamond is bad and we throw it away. So the greed (and all the defilements and conditions) has to be eradicated from our mind. Note: - without greed, we can still handle the diamond, use the diamond as necessary (to use only).

Defilements and conditions cannot function in the present moment (by moment). So we practice to quiet the mind – silent the mind and notice how peaceful and serene when we get to that stage.

(Here let me quote Patra Chakshuvej words after she went to Burma and meditate for one year – "I realized that the courageous effort that my teachers often emphasized has nothing to do with how much time one spends in the meditation hall or the duration of one's retreat. It is much more about developing the mental strength to view any situation without like or dislike and be able to see it for exactly what is: impermanent. It is about letting go of the past, not worrying about the future, and training the mind to stay exactly in the present moment)

(Please read on her personal experience about meditation and how it transformed her consciousness level by level)

You can find Patra Chakshuvej at her blog and web site: - Meditating in Myanmar blog entry. Panditarama Meditation Center website.

It is about letting go of the past, not worrying about the future, and letting the mind (gently and attentively) to stay in the present moment." When you realise and touch the nature of freedom (a taste of freedom) then you start to practice eradicating the defilements and conditions from the mind. This is the *Samatha* method. (*Samatha* meaning itself is tranquility or quiescence, not 'powers' as most wrongly understand) (Please see my book "Buddhism and Liberation")

When you understand the true nature of the things (that is they are *Anicca* - "inconstancy" or "impermanence", *Dukkha* – "dissatisfaction" or "suffering" and *Anatta* - "non-Self" or simply "no controlling factor") you release the psychological holding on them and be free (for a while first, in your meditation). The mind becomes peaceful and calm and indescribable happiness sets in – not that you got something; rather your mind is free from the bondage of the things and people.

On the other hand because of the *Samatha* method, your mind is in the present moment, peace and calm and indescribable happiness sets in. Same as above it is not that you obtain something; rather you are free from the bondage of the things and people.

Vipassanā is about developing 'Right View'. *Samatha* is to taste the freedom.

This stage which ever method you start is a must – the meditator(s) has to get to this stage. Teachers call it a taste of freedom – guessing the Nibbana (*Anumāna*). From that time on since you understand the true nature of your body and mind (*with Vipassana method*) or quietness of the mind – in the present moment, you start practicing to release all the defilements and conditions in the mind – and from the latent fields also. In this stage there is nothing to gain, nothing to get, just releasing the attachments, the clinging from the mind - eradicating all the psychological links from the worldly things and people. (Understanding the 1st and 2nd Noble Truth, Practicing the 4th Noble Truth – eradicating like in 3rd Noble Truth) You practice slowly and steady thus:-

The 'knowing mind' as 'thought processes' becomes crystal clear and pure, one-pointed and supple, you stay with the objects. The consciousness is *strong and clean*; simply being aware, noticing the objects – the psychological knots, that appeared through the senses. You did not entertain *nor* dismiss them away, simply acknowledging and letting them pass through the thought process. No thinking, no wandering, no sleeping, no trance - purely observing the objects passing by. Nothing tainted ***back*** into the feeling. Your consciousness is clear except that, the physical memory remained. ***There is no unfinished psychological data left in the memory (rather we should say nothing left in the feelings).*** The feelings are clean and pure. The mind is clean and pure, as it is, the mind as a mind as a mind, no more no less. No strong or weak, no master or slave, just assisting when needed.

There is no word of *Samatha* or *Vipassanā* in the Eightfold Path, but we can take as - Right Effort, Right Mindfulness, Right Concentration will quiet the mind (This leads to *Samatha* – Tranquility) and the Right View or Right understanding and Right Thought leads to *Vipassanā*, they both involved in the practicing. And the *Anapana-Sati* - Mindfulness of Breathing is to quiet the mind **naturally** with the breath – can be referred as *Samatha* method and *Mahā-Satipatthā-Sutta* - The Four Foundations of Mindfulness can be referred as *Vipassanā* method since it is discernment of the things, understanding.

But both of them ('Mindfulness of Breathing and the 'Four Foundations of Mindfulness) do not mention anything about the word *Vipassanā* and *Samatha*.

Just like I mentioned in my previous books that *Vipassanā* method all started in Burma and in 20th century and 21st century only, but they are very safe since they open the wisdom – understanding.

So whatever method you start they all come to complement each other, supporting each other, they go hand in hand.

But if one starts with *Vipassanā*, one needs to quiet the mind with the objects when they come in (Choice-less awareness or Bare Attention) without playing or entertaining them, simply stay with them and let them pass without affecting you. In the mean time try and understand the true nature of the things. Especially understand the body and mind as it is – they are <u>*Anicca*</u> - "inconstancy" or "impermanence", <u>*Dukkha*</u> – "dissatisfaction" or "suffering" and <u>*Anatta*</u> - "non-Self" or simply "no controlling factor") so that you can release the holding the body and mind. The mind becomes peace and calm and indescribable happiness sets in. You get the taste of freedom, and carry on with releasing the psychological attachments on the worldly things and people. You start the journey to the other side. Transcend to the other side - away from the defilements and conditioned side.

If one starts with the *Samatha* method, one needs to quiet the mind up to tranquility or quiescence, without playing or entertaining the objects when they come in through the senses. Simply stay with the main meditation object (such as in and out breath), let the mind be quiet and serene without being affected by the objects. The mind becomes peaceful and calm and indescribable happiness sets in. You get the taste of freedom and carry on with releasing the psychological attachments on the worldly things and people. You start the journey to the other side. Transcend to the other side. - away from the defilements and conditioned side.

This Eightfold Path is to be practiced along the journey to Liberation, so they are to be understood up to the level of Liberation. The mind should be clear of all the defilements and conditions, so all eight factors refer to the level of clear mind – the mind as it is.

(1) Right <u>view</u> (*Sammā-diṭṭhi*) can also be translated as "right perspective", "right outlook" or "right understanding"

We understand clearly without doubt that the unenlightened mind (and body) is in the suffering state, as pointed out in the First Noble Truth, we know the cause of the suffering as pointed in the Second Noble Truth and we have a clear view of what Liberation is. There is no doubt; we got the clear cut view of the whole practice – we process the journey to Liberation. As we tread the path, we got the map of our journey up to Liberation. The more we tread the clearer the path is. So Right View is all the way opening the wisdom (understanding) up to the 'Four Noble Truth'.

(2) Right Thought (*Sammā sankappa*) can also be known as "right intention", "right resolve", "right conception", "right aspiration"

There are two parts of mind process in the unenlightened mind.

(a) Thought processes.

(b) Thinking processes.

Thought processes are the normal process of the mind. When one is in deep sleep this 'thought process is doing its own job, without you participating. The thinking processes are from your part such as inventing, creating more than that if one is not liberated the thinking process -'For Me' creeps in just like I mentioned in chapter 2 - The Cause of Suffering – *Samudaya Sacca*.

In the prelude section I mentioned the 'Sense of Self'; here this 'Sense of Self' goes with the 'Right Thought' – 'good thinking process'. When we are hungry we look for food (in later life, we work and earn for a living – to get food). We do it with the 'Right Thought'. But when the bad 'Thinking process'- 'thinking For Me processes' comes in, all the cheating, stabbing in the back follows.

Right thoughts, when we start practicing, are described as good thinking (from your part) about doing the meritorious deeds, meditation, helping and so on. Also when in meditating, putting the mind to the meditation object (such as to the breathing) is the 'good thinking process.'

Advanced understanding about 'Right Thought': -

In spontaneous response stage, there is no 'Thinking process'. Thinking process and thought process merge together as spontaneous response – Thought Process. 'Thinking process' includes 'Time frame', past and future are there, you need time to think and there is also 'choice'. Calculating is there. That is why the bad thinking process – 'for me' can creep in.

There is no 'thinking process' in Kung Fu fighting, just spontaneous response, very beautiful, synchronizing with body and mind and it flows in the fighting. There is no time to think.

Like in 'Japanese Tea Ceremony' and 'Zen - the art of archery', there is no thinking process, just body and mind moving gracefully.

Moreover 'the Truth' – 'seeing the things as they truly are' cannot be realized through thinking or trying to figure it out. Either you see it or you do not see it. I already mentioned in my books that in *Nibbana* – Liberation state there is no mind. See the eminent meditation master 'Mahāsi Sayādaw' from Burma mentioning 'In *Nibbana* there are no such thing as consciousness or mental factors – and so on'. One Truth Only – A compilation of passages from his discourses book. First published in the Wheel Publication No. 298/299/300 as Thoughts on the *Dhamma*, Buddhist Publication Society, Kandy, Sri Lanka and later published by Inward Path Publisher, Penang, Malaysia.

In deep meditation, when the mind settles down, there is no thinking process just knowing mind as thought process – acknowledging the object(s) and letting them pass, there is no thinking about that object.

Enlightened persons do not need 'thinking process', not even 'good thinking process'. Since their mind is pure and clean, there is only spontaneous response.

So we practice unconditional response to spontaneous response. (See my book 'Buddhism and Liberation)

(3) Right speech (*Sammā-vācā*)

Normally we describe the 'Right speech as abstaining from lying, from divisive speech, from abusive speech, and from idle chattering. When practicing, we try and keep the moral conduct of right speech. Slowly when the mind is clean and pure, the 'Right Thought' takes care of the 'Right Speech'.

(4) Right action (*Sammā-kammanta*)

Cleaning the mind is its main job. With 'Right Action' we are careful (mindful) of the object when it comes in through the senses and not to turn it into attachment feeling(s) (up to desire and so on) and put it as psychological data. However when the links (of the object) make the past psychological data come up we are mindful about it and let it pass through, without putting it back in the memory.

Love can turn into hate. Love can turn into attachment. Both of this kind of love is done by the illusion of 'I', the *ATTA* – 'For Me', the 'EGO'. Even hurting or killing can turn into enjoyment like in some sports. According to Buddhism the past life of attachment in the feeling(s) is rolling in the mental formation when functioning.

Here comes the 'Right Action' – to make it right, to clear these satisfactions - attachment. *Kamma* (*lit*) is action.

When we have to take action, we must not shy away, back away or run away, nor to enjoy and become satisfied. We must go through them carefully and mindfully and not to turn them into feeling(s) – attachments and ***not to put it in the feeling - memory back again.*** If you turn away, this *Kamma* is not finished from the feeling and it is stored in the feeling (together with memory back) again.

The important thing is that whenever we do something we have to have "clear knowing", not to leave them as anger, hatred, jealously and so on (*in the feeling*). This is called 'Right Action'.

When you got the 'Right Thought', 'Right Action' flows in and *Kamma* is not accumulating, there is no unfinished psychological data in the feeling(s).

When we start practicing, this 'Right Action' is taking care of our morality – not killing, not stealing and so on. But later on when our practice goes deeper, it is like the above, not accumulating or impacting in the feeling.

Let me give you a good example:-

In ***Bhagavad Gītā*** (Hinduism teachings) in the section of The ***epics Mahābhārata*** (the big epic teaching about 'Man Kind' - 'Human Nature') there is a section, where ***Krishna*** was driving the chariot of ***Arjuna*** who is going for battle with his own relatives. *Arjuna* was reluctant to attack, since they were his relatives. *Krishna* explained that the *Kamma* is forming up now, if you turn away, run away, it will come back in different forms in the future. Go ahead and break through. You are the king, do your king's job, clear out this *Kamma*. The only thing is that you should be very careful not to let this turn into a war – killing turns to enjoyment – attachment to hurting (ego satisfaction) in your part, just simply do your job and ask no more. This is the time to clean up your past *Kamma*, an opportunity to clean this past *Kamma* once and for all.

In Hinduism, it is called the **Karma Yoga** – Cleaning the *Kamma*, letting the mind be clean and pure. This is the practice of 'Right Action'.

The Right Action is to practice unconditional response and spontaneous response in daily life. That is without longing for reward – psychological expectation(s). Without guilt, without remorse; the ending result is without 'FEAR' and finally it has to lead towards Non-attachment. In Buddhist terms we can say we function without greed, hatred and delusion. We understand the *Anicca* – non permanent, *Dukkha* – Suffering and *Anatta* – no controlling factors. When we realize these three characteristic of life and let go, we are free.

If you have family life, you do need to fulfill the commitment, fulfill your duty first. This is the 'Right Action'.

We are not supposed to be caught up in our comfort zone. Not abusing the body and mind (no drugs, alcohol, no intoxication). No laziness. The mind has to be sharp and clean enough to break through the past *Kamma* with Right Action.

Note: - In fact the entire Eightfold Path is to practice like the above.

(5) Right livelihood (*Sammā-ājīva*)

Right livelihood is having abandoned dishonest livelihood, our attitude towards harmless living. The types of businesses that are harmful to undertake are:

1. **Business in weapons**: trading in all kinds of weapons and instruments for killing.

2. **Business in human beings**: slave trading, prostitution, or the buying and selling of children or adults.

3. **Business in meat**: "meat" refers to breeding animals for slaughter.

4. **Business in intoxicants**: manufacturing or selling intoxicating drinks or addictive drugs.

5. **Business in poison**: producing or trading in any kind of toxic product designed to kill.

Here also, just like I mentioned in the prelude section, the 'Sense of Self' goes with the 'Right Thought'. When we are hungry we look for food (in later life, we work and earn for a living, to provide for food). We do it with the 'Right Thought'. But when the 'Thinking process' as 'For Me' comes in, all the cheating and back-stabbing comes in. We earn our living by working and living within our means, go together with the 'Right Thought'. Thus 'Right Livelihood is earning our living in the righteous way, without hurting other people. In short, we do not let the 'Thinking Process – "For Me" comes in, into our livelihood. This is the part where we try and get back to our 'Right Thought Process' in our 'Right Livelihood'.

When we practise these morality section of the eightfold path, there is no calculating 'for me' left in thoughts, words and deeds.

(6) Right effort (*Sammā-vāyāma*) can also be translated as "right endeavor"

Of course this section refers to the practice to be liberated. Buddha described the middle way as a path of moderation between the extremes of sensual indulgence and self-mortification. This, according to the Buddha, is the path of wisdom. The middle path does not mean a mid point in a straight line joining two extremes represented by points. The Middle Way is a dynamic teaching as shown by the traditional story that the Buddha realized the meaning of the Middle Way when he sat by a river and heard a 'lute' player in a passing boat and understood that the lute string must be tuned neither too tight nor too loose to produce a harmonious sound.

(Here the teacher is very responsible for the individual meditator to be in the 'Right Effort')

(7) Right mindfulness (*Sammā-sati*), also translated as "right awareness" or "right attention"

Sati (*lit.*) means 'Remembering' - to stay on the meditation object.

Bhikkhu Bodhi explains the concept of mindfulness as follows: The mind is deliberately kept at the level of *bare attention*, a detached observation of what is happening within us and around us in the present moment. In the practice of right mindfulness the mind is trained to remain in the present, open, quiet, and alert, contemplating the present event. All judgments and interpretations have to be suspended, or if they occur, just registered and dropped.

We trained our mind according to the **Satipaṭṭhāna** 'Four Foundation of Mindfulness' as taught by the Buddha. **Satipaṭṭhāna** refers to the establishing, foundation (*paṭṭhāna* or presence (*upaṭṭhāna*) of "mindfulness" (*sati*), in order to understanding the true nature of our selves and the nature.

(8) Right concentration (*Sammā-samādhi*), is the practice of concentration (*samadhi*)

Here we practise the mind to be stable, to be in the present moment. We cool it down, subside the wandering mind (outer and inner) so that the mind can

(1) Touch the 'Serene Nature' of the mind – a taste of freedom.

(2) To understand the true nature of the things.

This part of practicing is to march up together with the 'Right Understanding'.

The important thing is that we are not practicing to be slow in movement and become senile - it will transform you into veggie type or become Zombie. Actually we practice to synchronize body and mind, the precise movement towards the objects. It can be a slow movement, it can be fast (when needed), but there is always synchronization in every movement, so that our mind is sharp and clear (and clean) to understand the true nature of things.

In fact in walking meditation, the noting,(they all have to end up in synchronizing the body and mind) and the entire metabolism in the body and mind, should not become a zombie walking. The

'noting' in meditation should end up in quieting the mind, not to turn it into a habitual and mechanical noting.

The bottom line of this Eightfold Path is to practise the mind to be quiet, understand the true nature of things, release the *psychological* holdings (attachments) to the worldly things and people and be liberated.

Chapter 5

LANDMARKS.

I have repeatedly mentioned that meditation is not like passing an examination or following a step-by-step menu. It is just realization and releasing the attachments/cravings from the mind. Liberation is not a reward, not an achievement. It is not about stimulating the mind (to be high). It is not a status. It is not the result of anything. Nobody can give it to you (because it is not a thing); you cannot give it to anybody. You cannot explain precisely in words, but you can point out with our limited language. Even as we try to point out, the other person if he is not ready to accept and see (with wisdom eye), he will not be able to see or understand.

It is *indescribable happiness*. Here again, this happiness is not something you attained. It is because the mind is free (psychological) from all the bondage of the worldly things. In Buddhist words from the point of 3rd Noble Truth it is *the end of Suffering - Nirodha Sacca. The mind (and body) is free from the psychological holding to the things and people, such as craving, attachment.*

The journey is also not one by one free, not as step by step closer to Liberation – the *Nibbana*. But before you get to that enlightenment, the mind becomes lighter and lighter, more free, adapting (*Anuloma*) to the *Nibbana*. This is where the landmarks/ signs set in. You can feel the transformation of consciousness. Literary it means the consciousness change from 'For Me' process to 'Universal Process; 'Thinking Process' to 'Thought Process', just like I mentioned in Chapter 2 Page 9 and Chapter 4 Page 24. The journey is near ending, but when you arrive, you will know.

The following are the main landmarks in practicing the Four Noble Truths. They are landmarks in transformation of consciousness during the meditation. (It is not like Lights, or strange things, small super natural things or miracles encountered during the meditation. These are consciousness changing during meditation.

1. Serene and joy set in – in meditation. No problem in sitting. Body, mind and sitting synchronized.

2. Peaceful and indescribable happiness sets in.

3. Less psychological dependent.

4. Free from the past guilt or remorse and free from psychological expectation. (You are free from 'Psychological Time Frame') – Slowly you realize that you start to free from 31 existences.

5. Understanding the human nature, not with super natural powers, but with the clean, pure and free mind.

6. Your mind becomes the immeasurable - *Apramāṇa*, usually translated boundlessness, infinitude, a state that is illimitable. When developed to a high degree in meditation, these attitudes are said to make the mind "immeasurable" and like the mind of the loving *brahmā* (gods).

(a) You abide in four sublime states – *Brahmavihāra*; Love and kindness (wishing others to be happy), Compassion (removing suffering of ourselves and others), Empathetic joy (appreciating the success in others) and equanimity (accepting what is and allowing the heart to transcend that limitation)

Brahmavihāra means "*Brahma* abiding", or "sublime attitudes." It may be *parsed* as "*Brahma*" and "*vihāra*"; which is often rendered into English as "sublime" or "divine abodes"

(b) You will not be easily shaken by the eight worldly conditions – *Loka-Dhamma*. That is; Gain and Loss, Honor and Dishonor, Happiness and Misery, Praise and Blame. You are not too much concern about life and what will happen. You start to live day by day, asking for no more. You are in real *'Que Sera, Sera'* (Whatever will be, will be) mode.

7. Body and mind is stable and we know how to live and how to die.

You are not easily shaken by the worldly things and people. In fact the' Fear' is less and less. You dare to do what is right and suitable to help human beings. You know how to stay away from the corrupted people. You are *'Alone but not Lonely'* anymore. (If you are a monk or nun, you realize how advantage it is to wear robes and go for alms-food, it is practicing for less depending and psychological expectations) You know how to "Live ~ fully" and how to "Die ~ peacefully".

Chapter 6

CONCLUSION.

In the essay "Buddhism Meets Western Science" (you can find in Wikipedia – the free encyclopedia, the Eightfold Path section) Gay Watson explains:

Buddhism has always been concerned with feelings, emotions, sensations, and cognition. The Buddha pointed both to cognitive and emotional causes of suffering. The emotional cause is desire and its negative opposite, aversion. The cognitive cause is ignorance of the way things truly occur, or of three marks of existence: that all things are unsatisfactory, impermanent, and without essential self.

(Note: - I am not ascertain, conforming their mind as liberated mind, because I do not know the Liberated mind (yet), but you can see and feel the innocent, pure, natural, fresh and clean mind. It is not polluted; there is no calculating as 'For Me' thinking process)

The mind (and body) is free; neither master nor slave, assisting in functioning in this world – before passing away.

The bottom line of this Four Noble Truths is to understand the true nature of the things and relax, let it go – of the holdings to yourself (body and mind) and the people and things, the world,

the universe, especially holding on to craving- with intention or without intention to the 31 existence and free / Liberated.

Now we understand that there are two parts (journey through worldly things and journey through transcendental states). Buddhism is keen self-observation and helps us to realize who we really are. We do need to go (practice) through it, not like passing an exam, but to go through it.

Many traditions, many teachers but the core teaching remains the same, the gradual path of *Sila* (Morality), *Samadhi* (Concentration) and *Panna* (Wisdom) pointing to the same goal, the realization of *Nibbana* – the Liberation.

"You have to do your own work; Enlightened Ones only show the way"

This is what Buddhism and Buddhist meditation really are.

This is what 'Four Noble Truths' is.

Be happy, enjoy the journey - to Liberation!

About The Author

The Venerable Sayadaw U Khema Wuntha, Maha Thera holds a BA (Law) and LLB degree from the Burmese University in 1970 and 1971 respectively and was called to the Bar in 1972 and was admitted as an advocate and solicitor. He worked as a government law officer (Burma) from 1972 to 1976. He then practiced as a lawyer and migrated to the US in 1983. He was ordained in America as a Bhikkhu in 1985 under the Most Venerable Sayadaw U PANNA VAMSA, Chief Monk of Dhammikarama Burmese BuddhistTemple Penang and Chief monk of the Burmese Buddhist Temple in Los Angeles, America.

In 1990 Venerable Sayadaw U Khema Wuntha Maha Thera was stationed about a year in Toronto Burmese Temple giving talks and conducting Meditation retreat and thereafter was stationed back to Los Angeles.

Venerable Sayadaw was the Chief Resident Monk in Dhammikarama Buddhist Temple in Penang from 1996 to 2004. During that period Venerable was conducting meditation classes, Abidhamma study, Dhamma talks and mass ordination of novice monks and *samaneras.*

Venerable Sayadaw was the Chief Monk in Ratana-Rama Buddhist Temple under MMBA, Kuala Lumpur. Venerable Sayadaw conducted meditation classes, conducted ordination, taught Abhidhamma and gave Dhamma talks during his stay there.

Venerable Sayadaw also gave Dhamma talks, discussions and conducted meditation classes at Chempaka Buddhis Lodge, Section 24 in Petaling Jaya and many other meditation centers including those in Miri and Sibu.

Venerable Sayadaw was based at Sasana Ransi Buddhist Temple in Frankfurt, Germany between 2007 and 2008, helped to established the temple. Also to conduct meditation classes and Dhamma talks.

In April 2008, Venerable Sayadaw was stationed back in Dhammikarama Buddhist Temple in Penang as the Chief Residing Monk.

In 2009 he was stationed back in Burmese Buddhist Temple in Los Angeles, America.

In 2011 he was stationed in Burmese Buddhist Temple under Burmese Buddhist Association, Chicago, USA as a residing monk till to-date.

He has published four Buddhism books in English and two Buddhism books in Burmese and numerous articles.

Venerable Sayadaw also attended a number of Buddhist conferences, travelled widely throughout the world.

You can reach Sayadaw U Khema Wuntha at :-

Cell Phone: (630)9913609 Email : - kwuntha@yahoo.com